Grand Central Station: The History of New York City's Famous Railroad Terminal

By Charles River Editors

Luigi Novi's picture of Grand Central Terminal

About Charles River Editors

Charles River Editors provides superior editing and original writing services across the digital publishing industry, with the expertise to create digital content for publishers across a vast range of subject matter. In addition to providing original digital content for third party publishers, we also republish civilization's greatest literary works, bringing them to new generations of readers via ebooks.

Sign up here to receive updates about free books as we publish them, and visit Our Kindle Author Page to browse today's free promotions and our most recently published Kindle titles.

Introduction

Picture of the main concourse

Grand Central Station

"In Grand Central you cannot shilly shally or dilly dally. Everyone rushes and dashes and zips and zaps and whizzes like crazy and oh what a dizzy and delightful place." - Maira Kalman, *Next Stop Grand Central*

Of all the great cities in the world, few personify their country like New York City. As America's largest city and best known immigration gateway into the country, the Big Apple represents the beauty, diversity and sheer strength of the United States, a global financial center that has enticed people chasing the "American Dream" for centuries.

Given that background, it's fitting that the city's most iconic railroad station, Grand Central Terminal, is the largest in the world, sprawling across nearly 50 acres with over 40 platforms and 65 lines. Moreover, in addition to handling hordes of bustling commuters, it's now a classic tourist spot that attracts tens of millions of visitors annually. As author Tom Wolfewould so eloquently put it, "Every big city had a railroad station with grand — to the point of glorious — classical architecture — dazzled and intimidated, the great architects of Greece and Rome would have averted their eyes — featuring every sort of dome, soaring ceiling, king-size column, royal cornice, lordly echo — thanks to the immense volume of the spaces — and the miles of marble, marble, marble — but the grandest, most glorious of all, by far, was Grand Central Station."

Like Manhattan itself, Grand Central Station, which recently celebrated its 100th birthday, manages to be both historic and modern. Built upon the site of a former railroad depot, the current structure and layout was phased in over the course of nearly a decade in the early 20th century. Whereas the first railroad stations depressed the value of land nearby in the 19th century, the location of Grand Central was a boon that actually helped bring about construction all across Midtown, including the nearby Chrysler Building, thereby serving to transform the cityscape altogether.

As Central Station took on increasing importance, the cultural significance of the terminal also changed as New Yorkers began to look at the place as a work of art itself. Grand Central has since been stocked with art in all shapes and sizes, with galleries that call it home and special events being held there. Thus, when proposed changes or even possible replacements for Grand Central were bandied about in the 1960s, they met widespread opposition, including from former First Lady Jackie Kennedy, who asked, "Is it not cruel to let our city die by degrees, stripped of all her proud monuments, until there will be nothing left of all her history and beauty to inspire our children? If they are not inspired by the past of our city, where will they find the strength to fight for her future? Americans care about their past, but for short term gain they ignore it and tear down everything that matters. Maybe… this is the time to take a stand, to reverse the tide, so that we won't all end up in a uniform world of steel and glass boxes." As a result, Grand Central was maintained as a landmark and has instead undergone restorations.

Grand Central Station: The History of New York City's Famous Railroad Terminal chronicles the construction and history of the Big Apple's most famous park. Along with pictures of important people, places, and events, you will learn about Grand Central like never before, in no time at all.

Grand Central Station: The History of New York City's Famous Railroad Terminal

About Charles River Editors

Introduction

Chapter 1: The Story of Urban America

"The story of Grand Central mirrors the story of urban America. It is a story that reveals the secrets of hidden staircases, mysterious underground vaults, a publicity-shy owner, and a secluded platform reserved for the president of the United States. It is a story about people, from Bryan Henry, a Metro-North cop who befriended the homeless, to Audrey Johnson, who fields customers' questions in the information booth, to Jacqueline Onassis, whose devotion to historic preservation saved the terminal from certain destruction. Grand Central has been the wellspring of new beginnings for millions of people who arrived in New York to fulfill their dreams, heeded the siren call to go west, and returned lovesick to their hometowns. Unlike a station, a terminal conjures up a destination, not merely a place to pass through. Grand Central embodied that role, as the gateway to New York since 1913 and as the city's Gateway to a Continent. Between 1913 and the centennial of the New York Central in 1926, the number of passengers served annually by the terminal nearly doubled, to 43 million from 23 million. Today, the number is verging on a record, headed, for the first time, toward the 100 million passengers a year forecast when the terminal first opened a century ago." – Sam Roberts, *Grand Central: How a Train Station Transformed America*

New York City is one of those places that always seemed destined for greatness. Colonized along with much of the rest of the East Coast of North America during the 17th century, it quickly rose to become a center of commerce and travel, owing largely to its sheltered harbors and moderate climate. When trains were introduced as a popular means of transportation, some of the first tracks laid terminated in New York, and the expansion of railroads led to the birth of train stations across the country. In general, these were small buildings where passenger could buy tickets and wait for their trains to arrive, and according an article written by Samuel Dunn around the turn of the 20th century, "The first Manhattan terminal was opened in 1832 at Centre Street, near the present City Hall, by the New York and Harlem road, now leased to the New York Central. Trains were run by steam as far south as Fourteenth Street and pulled from there by horses." If it is hard to conceive of large box cars or even heavier locomotives being pulled by horse, it's important to remember that the first train cars were little more than traditional carriages designed to move on iron tracks.

Through the years, the trains got bigger and the number of passengers they carried increased with them, so another station was completed in 1857 on the site that now houses Madison Square Garden. The New York Depot became the point where trains from numerous lines converged in one spot, and this dingy depot that provided shelter for those coming and going became its own small Ellis Island as immigrants attempted to understand how much money they needed to get to relatives all across the country. The Civil War also saw thousands of soldiers shipped through the station, with the healthy ones going south to fight and the wounded ones coming home to recover. All of this took its toll, especially on the value of the land in the area, since no one wanted to live near the depot. In 1867, the famous newspaperman Horace Greeley observed,

"We lived on this road when it was poor and feebly managed —with rotten cars and wheezy old engines that could not make schedule time; and the improvement since realized is gratifying... With an underground track from the Battery to Harlem Flats, its passenger fares would be speedily doubled. Such a track 10 years ago would have kept thousands in our state who have been driven over to Jersey by the full hour now required to traverse the space between City Hall and the Harlem River. With a good underground railroad, the census of 1880 will credit Westchester County with a population of at least half a million, whereof at least 50,000 will visit our city daily."

By this time, Cornelius Vanderbilt was at the height of his power and in control of many of the trains that came through the depot, but the self-made mogul was not especially popular with the general public. One particularly unkind article around that time complained, "Each new million that he seized was an additional resource by which he could bribe and manipulate; progressively his power advanced; and it became ridiculously easier to get possession of more and more property... the mere threat of pitting his enormous wealth against competitors whom he sought to destroy was generally a sufficient warrant for their surrender." While his activities may not have been as illegal as this author thought, he was determined to wipe out as many of his competitors as possible, and to that end, he decided to build his own depot in New York and create something that would attract more customers to his trains.

Vanderbilt

Of course, not everyone was thrilled, especially those living in the stylish neighborhood around St. John's Park that Vanderbilt chose for his first large terminal. Railroad enthusiast Edward Hungerford later wrote, "Some New Yorkers who clung wistfully to the thought of open spaces with green lawns and stately trees here and there throughout their city protested, but they were laughed out of court. The trees were razed, the park leveled, and workmen were laying the foundations of the new freight house almost before New York knew just what was being done." At its heart stood a 12 foot tall statue of Vanderbilt himself, complete with an overcoat that one journalist called, "ample to protect from frost a Siberian sledge driver." In the same vein, after visiting the site of the new depot, George Templeton Strong wrote in his diary, "Have inspected the grand $ 800,000 Vanderbilt bronze. It's a 'miscellaneous billing' of cog-wheels, steamships, primeval forests, anchors, locomotives, piraguas ('pettyaughers,' we called them when I was a boy), R.R. Trains, wild ducks (or possibly seagulls) & squatter shanties, with a colossal Cornelius Vanderbilt looming up in the midst of the chaos, & beaming benignantly down on

Hudson Street, like a Pater Patriae— draped in a dressing gown or an overcoat, the folds whereof are most wooden. As a work of art, it is bestial."

Those who complained were silenced with reminders that this was progress and should be welcomed, not censored. One article in support asserted, "Railroads being the great means of commerce should be encouraged, not obstructed, and if the fuel of the pipe or the smoke of the locomotive was to be considered a cause of nuisance, that the steamboats should be banished from our seas and rivers, or silenced whenever they come so near a city to be heard."

Even with support for railroad terminals, there was the problem of what to do regarding the confusion that came with having so many different trains from different companies pulling into different stations. Visitors to the city often missed their trains because they went to the wrong station, and those attempting to send their luggage ahead were taking a terrible chance since it was easy for things to be delivered to the wrong station. In 1869, one paper noted that "the thousands of strangers daily arriving here from all directions have been dumped in the open streets, or, at best, landed in some old dilapidated shed, and then left to the tender mercies of heartless hackmen, rowdy runners, and other sharks that prey upon strange visitor."

Realizing that there was money to be made in solving this problem, Vanderbilt came up with the idea of a central location at which all the trains coming into the city could converge. Given the problems inherent in the current system, the public was more enthusiastic about this project. At least one person was already envisioning a station befitting the splendor of New York City, writing, "People who come to New York should enter a palace on the end of their ride, and not a shed. The stranger who visits us for business or pleasure should be impressed by the magnificence of the great city upon his very entrance within its limits. So we endorse Mr. Vanderbilt's proposed depot on 41st street. Let it be worthy of him and of the metropolis."

Vanderbilt began by buying as much land as he could get his hands on between 42nd and 48th streets in the area between Lexington and Madison Avenues. When interviewed about his plans, he explained his plan to create a depot with three train stations under one roof. It would also have a large area in back for loading and unloading freight. The press loved his plan, with *The Sun* saying it was "a source of gratification and pride to our own citizens, to learn that this mortifying omission in the appointments for the reception and care of the throngs of guests constantly arriving and departing is to exist no longer. Commodore Vanderbilt, whose word is law in such matters, has decreed that New York shall have the most spacious, elegant, and convenient depot to be found in the country. And having issued the decree, the work of construction commences at once, hundreds of laborers and mechanics rushing at the call of the sturdy and enterprising old monarch to expedite the work."

Chapter 2: After the Tracks Were Buried

"When the depot first opened, the 100 trains that clattered over the Fourth Avenue tracks every day made such a racket that classes at Columbia College on 49th Street were disrupted. After the tracks were buried, though, Edith Wharton, who lived in a town house on Park at 78th Street, wrote to a friend in 1896 that in any given hour, 'seven or eight trains passed without affecting our nervous system. What happens is a short roar & rumble, & a puff of white smoke'…The tunnel pleased neighbors and pedestrians, but not passengers of the three railroads served by the depot. By 1880, Manhattan's population would approach 1.2 million, and with Tammany politicians and their cronies profiting from paving contracts and real estate booms, the street grid that was first plotted on paper long before, in 1811, was finally wending its way north of what would become known as Midtown. By 1900, the population would top 1.8 million, and the grand depot, which had seemed so durable only three decades earlier and which the Commodore figured would suffice for a century, had devolved into a hopeless anachronism incapable of accommodating its 15 million passengers a year— much less future growth." – Sam Roberts, *Grand Central: How a Train Station Transformed America*

As is often the case, progress requires sacrifice, and in the case of Grand Central, that meant replacing preexisting structures to make room for the terminal. Many New Yorkers were saddened to hear that the charming Church of the Resurrection was going to be torn down to make way for the new depot, and in December 1869, *The Sun* complained, "Neither private interests, the claims of churches, asylums, public markets, nor any other obstacle, baulks the old veteran when he undertakes a job of this kind. … He goes quietly to the Legislature and reinforces himself with such special enactments as he desires, and being thus fully prepared enters upon his grand schemes, regardless of whatever opposition may present itself."

Nonetheless, the station that John Snook designed was elegantly L-shaped with three large towers topped by round domes reminiscent of those in Tsarist Russia. Each dome topped its own depot, with a center tower rising 12 stories from the ground. Once inside, passengers could proceed to any of the three "separate and exclusive apartments, both as to waiting rooms, ticket offices, baggage rooms and so on, and each finding ample accommodation in the upper stories for its general offices." The building itself was 600 by 200 feet and covered with an arched glass ceiling more than 110 feet above. Throughout the building ran 12 separate train tracks, each raised to the level of the surrounding sidewalks, and perhaps the most amazing thing about the new depot was how the cars arrived in it. No coal burning, soot producing engines were allowed inside, so the engine separated from the cars as it approached and pulled on to a siding, allowing the passenger cars to coast into the depot.

Snook

Snook's design for the Grand Central Depot

When the Grand Central Depot opened on October 9, 1871, *The Sun* conceded that it was worth the bother: "The handling of nearly one hundred trains both arriving and departing daily, it will be readily apprehended, will require much space and the ground here taken for that purpose will be none too extensive." However, the railroad began to outgrow Grand Central Depot immediately after it opened, and according to *The Times*, the people of New York "denounced the administration of affairs, not only in regard to the slow and wretched arrangement of time on the horse-cars, but also the inconveniences and outrages suffered by passengers at the Grand Central Depot ." One commuter complained that a trip downtown took twice as long as before because "we lose one hour between the depot and City Hall."

Pictures of Grand Central Depot

Others disagreed, and one individual claimed it was "the finest passenger railroad depot in the world," but either way, the value of Grand Central Depot was largely in the eye of the beholder. For instance, while it did serve a much needed purpose and significantly improved the lives of both long and short term travelers, the depot's layout proved to be somewhat menacing to its patrons. In 1871, *The Times* called the area around the depot a "most fearful death-trap," adding that at "this now populous quarter…[one] has but to stand a few minutes in 45th Street, where the cars enter and pass out of the depot, to see the peril to which life is daily put, and to wonder that more people are not wounded or killed for their temerity in attempting a crossing. … There is a continual ringing of bells and screaming of whistles that is confusing to the senses, awakened to the possibility of danger from an unknown or unseen quarter."

The *New York Tribune* also reported about the danger: "City Sanitary Inspector Morris presented a report complaining that the Grand Union Depot is dangerous to life. He said that the network of tracks from Forty-fifth to Fifty-Fourth St is crowded with cars, which obstruct the view of approaching trains, and that many accidents have happened since the opening of the depot, partly in consequent of the additional number of trains sent out each hour. He stated that within the past twelve days seven persons have lost their lives by being run over by trains approaching or leaving this depot."

Eventually, this issue was addressed well enough that in 1874, *Scientific American* carried an article in which it noted, "It is gratifying to know that rapid transit in this great city is making real progress. The magnificent line of solid and substantial underground railways on Fourth Avenue, between the Grand Central Depot, 42nd street, and Harlem River… authorized by the State Legislature of 1872, is now almost completed, and will open for traffic in January next. The continuation of these tracks down town to the southern limit of the city, at the Battery, 4.J miles, by the Broadway Underground Railway Company, was finally authorized by the Legislature, May 10, 1874; and although but a brief time has elapsed, it is believed that the construction will soon begin. These great works…built in the strongest manner, under the direct supervision of the most eminent engineers, will form a rapid transit railway of which the citizens of New York may well be proud. Our engineers will do well to lend all possible influence in favor of their early completion. Over these tracks, passengers may be safely conveyed, at high velocity and for low fares. Nothing about these roads will be experimental or uncertain. Their capacity for traffic will be enormous; they will in all respects be adequate, convenient, and satisfactory to the public."

To his credit, Vanderbilt also provided for the needs of his employees, believing that happier employees would do better jobs. In the basement of the depot there were rooms "comfortably fitted up" where, according to *The Times*, those on breaks could "indulge in profitable reading or conversation or amuse themselves with music. A library has been gradually built up and the books are allowed to be taken by the members to their homes for short periods." Families were also invited to join employees during the holidays for parties, and *The Times* reported that at a Christmas party in 1871, there was a special dinner and that "the fare is the best that the market affords, every kind of meat being provided, from mutton to venison. ... During this time yesterday 400 meals were served by a bevy of pretty young women, the wives, sisters, or daughters of the members of the association. During the afternoon there was a chorus singing at intervals, and in the evening a very pleasant musical entertainment was given by members of the association."

Following complaints about the smoke and noise the trains made, Vanderbilt teamed up with the city to dig tunnels through which many of the trains could approach the stations, but this upset plenty of people. By 1889, the Railway Gazette reported, "The Grand Central yard is now one of the most crowded in the country...Engines are flying around in so many directions that injuries to employees are somewhat frequent, and no financial obstacles should stand in the way of the substantial abatement of the confusion now existing." Another New Yorker complained that "someone living on East 46th Street near Third Avenue , and wishing to go to 46th Street and Fifth Avenue, has to go to 42nd Street or 49th Street, making a detour of a half mile because this monopoly has made it unsafe to cross at any other point. ... There is no single thing on New York Island so dangerous to the community and prejudicial to its interests as this Valley of the Shadow of Death, which cuts the city in two its entire length, and stretches, unpaved, ungraded, and is given over to the hundreds of locomotives that continually dash up and down, through the richest district of New York."

Chapter 3: Doubts About the Depot's Adequacy

"Had there been any doubts about the depot's adequacy even after the renovations, two events dispelled them as the new century began. The fatal crash in the Grand Central yards prompted demands that the engineer and even the New York Central's management be prosecuted for manslaughter and suggestions that the railroad be barred from Manhattan altogether and required to build a new terminus at its Mott Haven yards in the South Bronx instead. A month earlier, another event proved just as decisive: the Pennsylvania Railroad, the New York Central's chief competitor to points west, announced that it would challenge the Central's Manhattan monopoly by tunneling under the Hudson River from New Jersey and building a sumptuous station on the West Side. ... Central. The fatal 1902 crash persuaded him that the renovations, as impressive as they were, were insufficient to stem the rising tide of public outrage over the preposterous notion of running a chaotic railroad yard in what a few decades earlier had been a practically bucolic landscape but by now was becoming the very heart of the nation's largest city." – Sam Roberts, *Grand Central: How a Train Station Transformed America*

Pictures of the exterior and interior of Grand Central Depot in 1904

ONE END OF THE WAITING ROOM, GRAND CENTRAL STATION, NEW YORK.

A 1901 picture of the waiting room in Grand Central Depot

It was common knowledge in railroad circles and elsewhere that Vanderbilt operated his trains primarily to make a profit, but in turn, he understood that making a profit required keeping the public happy. Thus, Vanderbilt constantly attempted to upgrade the systems in the depot to make them safer and more efficient. In 1890, the *Scientific American* reported, "The yard of the Grand Central Depot, in New York, has recently been equipped with a new interlocking switch and signal system. Four parallel lines of tracks enter the yard at its northern end, and as they approach the two depot buildings fork and diverge until twenty-one lines of parallel tracks are produced. Trains from three separate railroads enter and leave the depot, involving between two and three thousand train movements daily. … In a central building called the tower a number of levers are placed. These are connected to rods running along the tracks, some for operating switches, others for rotating signals. When a lever is pulled in one direction or the other, it therefore moves the corresponding switch or lever. The levers are made to interlock with each other, so that certain levers can only be moved after others have been operated. In this way their movements are made interdependent and have to follow certain and definite orders of movement, which are susceptible of any desired variation. When the order of movement of a set of levers has been fixed by the adjustment of the interlocking mechanism, it cannot be departed from in operation."

Unfortunately, the new signals were not perfect, and on February 20, 1891, a horrific accident took place near the depot. According to *The Evening World*, "At 7:15 the 7:05 New Haven local passenger train, north bound, approached the station at Eighty-Sixth Street. A mist filled the tunnel and the light had partially failed because of the storm of snow and hail which had lasted all morning. A train of sleeping cars was ahead on the same track as the New Haven train. This was run into by the New Haven local, which was going at a high rate of speed. The crash was terrific, and both trains, engines and cars, were completely telescoped and smashed to atoms. The cars of the forward train caught fire from a stove, and the flames rose high above the wreck. Two alarms of fire were sent out, followed immediately by two calls for ambulances. The latter were responded to by four ambulances from the Presbyterian hospital. When the police, doctors and firemen reached the scene they found approach difficult by reason of the complete wreck of the cars, combined with the smoke, flames and the narrow limits of the tunnel. Groans from injured, and apparently dying people added to the terror to the scene."

To make matters worse, the train that caused the accident was one of the company's own. The article continued, "At 9 o'clock it was believed that ten dead or dying were still under the wreck. Officials of the New York and New Haven Railroad gave the following statement: 'The…train was a "shop train," composed of seven Boston and Albany cars, bound for the yard at Mott Haven, which left the Grand Central station at 7 A.M. The collision occurred near Eighty-Sixth Street, In the Fourth avenue tunnel. It was with another train going on the same track, and the first train ran into it from behind. The last car of the forward train took fire.' It was not then known how many passengers were killed, as other passengers were still supposed to be buried in the wreck. The smash-up was so complete that the doctors consider it scarcely within the bounds of possibility that any could come out of it with chances of life. The wreck blocked all traffic for several hours."

This accident drew attention to an ongoing problem with the Grand Central Depot, namely that by the end of the 19th Century, it was showing its age. On top of that, the depot was increasingly incapable of keeping up with the increasing amount of rail traffic being routed through it each day. Architect Bradford Gilbert, who designed Central Station in Chicago, made some improvements to the facility in 1898, but this was largely a stopgap measure, and the following year, *The Times* asserted, "Nothing pertaining to New York City except its government has been so discreditable to it as its principal railroad station. … The ugly structure has been a cruel disgrace to the metropolis and its inhabitants."

Gilbert

Another accident on January 8, 1902 proved to be the final straw. That day the tunnel at Grand Central was "[u]nusually murky" owing to the cold, wet weather, "the kind of weather that would make smoke or vapor hang in the air a long time without being shattered." Engineer John Wisker pushed his engine hard, running through the tunnel at a fast 35 miles per hour, and though there were lights along his path urging caution, he either did not see them or simply ignored them. Whatever the case, by the time he saw the red light indicating there was another train on his track, it was too late, and he wound up slamming into the rear of another commuter train, instantly killing 15 passengers and injuring another 36, two of whom died later that week. One survivor later recalled, "The hissing steam and smoke made it seem that I was going to be cooked alive." According to a *New York Times* article published on January 9, 1902, "Fifteen persons were killed and two score severely injured as a result of a rear-end collision in the Park Avenue railroad tunnel, at Fifty-sixth Street, yesterday morning at 8:20 o'clock. Unaccountable blunders of an engineer, who disregarded signals, which he says he did not see, are held to be responsible for the accident -- the worst railroad disaster that ever occurred on Manhattan Island…That a terrible tragedy had occurred was evident immediately. Above the hissing of escaping steam could be heard shrieks and groans of pain. There was a din of breaking glass and crackling woodwork. The boiler of the engine was inside the wrecked car. Dead and wounded were on each side and in front of this boiler, filled as it was with boiling water and steam. The force of the engines' impact had telescoped the rear car on to the car ahead. The passengers who were sitting in the forward portion of the car, therefore, were pushed backward. Those sitting in the rear were plunged upward and forward. Only a space of some nine feet remained between the headlight of the engine and the platform of the second car...The damage done to those in the rear train and in the forward cars of the Danbury train was largely due to fright. A few were bruised or cut, but many fainted and suffered severe nervous shocks. As soon as could be, the men who maintained presence of mind opened the doors of the other cars and enabled the passengers to alight. The tunnel was so filled with fumes, however, that little could be seen one way or another."

A picture of part of the damage caused by the crash

The accident made headlines across the country, and the *Chicago Daily Tribune* was concerned about what had gone wrong and who was to blame: "The disregarding of block signals by the engineer of a train was responsible for a collision in the New York Central tunnel today and resulted in the death of fifteen persons and the serious injury of sixteen others, at least two of whom are not expected to survive. John Wischo [sic], the engineer is under arrest, bail being refused, pending full inquiry into the disaster. He is in a state of collapse, and the only explanation he can give is that he was trying to make up lost time when his engine plowed its way through the crowded passenger coach of a train which had stopped in the tunnel...Most of the death, injury, and damage was wrought by the engine of the White Plains train, which plunged into the rear car of the motionless train and was driven through to the middle of the car, smashing the seats and furnishings and splitting the sides as it moved forward. The victims either were mangled in the mass of wreckage carried at the pilot, crushed in the space between boiler and car sides, or scalded by steam which came from broken pipes and cylinders."

Anxious to establish blame, *The Times* noted, "As slowly the harvest of death reaped in the hole under the New York streets is being garnered in the homes of New Rochelle, the townsmen of the dead and the maimed are beginning to ask each other not how this thing occurred, but why." *The Brooklyn Daily Eagle* reported, "District Attorney Jerome continued his official investigation today into causes of the disaster in the New York Central tunnel yesterday afternoon, which caused the death of fifteen persons and injuries to at least forty. A number of employees of the railroad company was summoned by the district Attorney to appear before him. The scene of the calamity in the tunnel continues to exercise a strange fascination for the morbidly minded. All night long, although there was absolutely nothing to be seen but the bare, dark opening of the tunnel, a curious crowd lingered around the spot and discussed in awe-struck whispers the fatality which had wiped out fifteen lives and injured scores of men and women."

Even worse, at least from the Vanderbilt family's perspective, there were rumors that the company heads might be prosecuted for negligent homicide. As District Attorney William Jerome later said, "It was not enough that the New York Central Railroad had been maintaining for many years a defective signal system and that any day a serious accident might happen as a result of the maintenance of such a system but it must have been found affirmatively, and beyond reasonable doubt, that this particular accident, with the ensuing deaths, occurred as the direct result of its defective system." Ultimately, however, the state chose not to prosecute, and the remedy would be one that looked forward, not backwards. Within days, plans were being discussed for a new and better facility.

Chapter 4: Two Daunting Challenges

"Once he was given the go-ahead, Wilgus still faced two daunting challenges: how to electrify the railroad (and how much of it to electrify); and how to build a new terminal and raze the old one without disrupting passenger traffic. He approached both quandaries with characteristic bravado. Rather than adhere narrowly to the mandate imposed by the state— to ban steam locomotives in Manhattan— Wilgus proposed to electrify the railroad the full 23 miles to White Plains on the Harlem line and all 33 miles to Croton on the Hudson line. He gave two compelling reasons. One was that commuters accounted for a growing proportion of the railroad's passenger traffic and they would be reluctant to waste time transferring in the Bronx to steam locomotives. Moreover, as noted, electric motors allowed trains to accelerate more quickly than steam locomotives, a big advantage for commuter railroads that hopscotched between suburban stations. Theoretically, what Wilgus was proposing seemed sensible, and the decision, as he later described it, was 'inescapable.' But translating his hypotheses about the technological and commercial advantages of electricity into dependable motive power was something else altogether." – Sam Roberts, *Grand Central: How a Train Station Transformed America*

On January 21, 1905, the *Scientific American* discussed the aging Grand Central Depot and a potential replacement: "In planning the truly magnificent station which is to take the place of the present Grand Central Station of the New York Central Railroad, the company have shown a full appreciation of the magnitude of the problem and of the inexorable necessity that is laid upon them of building not merely for today, but for the vast increase of travel of the far future. When the present structure was built, back in the seventies, it was the wonder of the day; and because of its magnitude, its great arch of glass and iron, its many parallel tracks, its long stretch of office buildings, and other features of greatness, the Grand Central Station was, for many years, an object of much civic pride in New York city. It was built with a strict eye to the future; nevertheless, but two decades had passed when the company began to realize that so rapid was the increase in traffic, that their great station was great no longer, and that before long they must begin to pull down and build on a far more generous scale. The question of enlargement was receiving serious consideration, when the enormous inconvenience, not to say danger, attending the running of steam-operated trains through the tunnel approach to the station became so acute, that legislative powers were sought to enable the company to dispense with steam locomotives altogether, and operate the terminal yard and the suburban traffic by electrical traction. The opportunity presented by this change of motive power enabled the company at the same time to greatly enlarge and entirely reconstruct the station yard and the terminal buildings."

The *Scientific American* article went on to introduce its reader to the plans for the new station: "The magnificent structure…is the outcome of a continuous study of the problem by the architects, Messrs. Warren & Wetmore, associated with Messrs. Reed & Stem, and by the engineering staff of the New York Central Company. Every possible arrangement of tracks and type of building was considered, and no less than two hundred different sets of plans are now on file in the architects' office, as evidence of the care with which the problem was studied. The present designs were adopted because they conform to certain important principles which were laid down as indispensable to the successful operation of a great terminal station such as this…."

One of the men who contributed heavily to the design and construction of the new terminal was William Wilgus. As Sam Roberts pointed out, "William Wilgus was an engineer, not an architect, but he hoped to impose his own aesthetic on the new terminal. He knew what he didn't like about the old depot: its 'unattractive architectural design' and its 'unfortunate exterior color treatment,' as well as the 'great blunder' of dividing the city for 14 blocks and by obstructing Fourth Avenue. Once he persuaded the Vanderbilts and the Central's other directors to accept his bold vision, they were intent on not repeating earlier mistakes, which had cost not only money, but goodwill as well."

Wilgus

Fortunately for Wilgus, his brother-in-law's firm, Reed and Stem, was one of the two chosen to build the terminal. The other firm, Warren and Wemore, was owned by one of Vanderbilt's cousins. Reed and Stem handled design while Warren and Wetmore created the architectural features and gave the building its overall Beaux-Arts look. When he resigned in 1907, W. C. Brown, then a senior vice-president with the railroad, wrote, "The great work undertaken and practically completed by you, of changing the power within the so-called electric zone and the reconstruction of the Grand Central Station, was the most stupendous work of engineering I have ever known; and it has gone forward practically without a halt, certainly without a failure in any essential feature."

There were indeed five important principles that the architects considered. The first concerned the impression that the station would make on visitors, because by the turn of the 20th century, New York City had come to symbolize the quintessential American metropolis. Wilgus later wrote about some of his suggestions, one of which involved building a multistoried building on top of the new terminal, and that one of his colleagues "felt that the office space would be a place only 'for birds to roost'; that the proposed hotel on the vacant square bounded by Madison Avenue, 43rd and 44th Streets and Vanderbilt Avenue, would be as unpopular as railroad hotels in Europe; that…cab-men could not be driven to use Madison Avenue because of their addiction to the sights of Fifth Avenue; and that underground horse cab-stands would be repulsive because of odors. My counter-arguments were that the rapidly increasing demand for office space in the vicinity would surely bring us tenants; that the use of electricity would obviate the features that made the European railroad hotels unpopular; that growing congestion would cause the cab-man to gladly avail himself of the new thoroughfares; and that the coming of the motor-car, then in its infancy, instead of the horse-drawn vehicle would obviate objectionable odors. It was also necessary to urge counter-arguments against the allegations of those who were not friendly to ramps in place of stairways and who opposed what they termed the 'grocery store' idea of lending the station to revenue producing purposes."

In the end, the final plans deviated from Wilgus' vision, as noted by the author of the *Scientific American* article: "The station must be considered as a great gateway to the city and, therefore, must be simple and dignified in its architecture, and must provide the broadest possible facilities for the inflow and outflow of traffic. It was this consideration that condemned those plans which contemplated the erection above the station of a vast office building; for such a structure would have congregated several thousand people at the very point where it was desired to provide a broad unobstructed thoroughfare for incoming and outgoing passengers."

The latter was a critical decision since the combination of high land values and new, stronger types of building materials made New Yorkers very inclined to build up rather than out, while the second consideration came in light of concerns about public safety that had plagued Grand Central Depot from its inception. The author explained, "The progress of the passengers from the street to the cars and from the cars to the street, must take place as far as possible in two direct and entirely separated channels; the incoming and outgoing crowds never meeting or intermingling with those moving in the opposite direction." This final point was crucial because it would keep people moving in the same direction and cut down on the amount of confusion in the station. Likewise, as the article noted, "In passing from the street to the cars, the passenger should take the steps incidental to departure in their natural consecutive order, with as little running to and fro as possible; the waiting room, the ticket office, the baggage room, the concourse, and the departing platform presenting themselves successively to him as he moves to his particular train. Similarly, the incoming passenger should find the incoming baggage room, the cab stand, and the means of exit to subway station or to street, presented to him in quick and logical succession."

A picture of excavation being done in 1908

Engraved by G. W. Peters. Half-tone plate engraved by C. W. Chadwick
SCENE IN THE EXCAVATION FOR THE NEW GRAND CENTRAL STATION
OF THE NEW YORK CENTRAL RAILWAY (LOOKING SOUTH)

A 1907 depiction of the excavation work

A picture of the construction of Grand Central Station in progress

The next consideration was one that was becoming increasingly important as more and more New Yorkers left the downtown area to move to the suburbs. "The express and long-distance passengers, whose progress through the station either in departing or arriving is necessarily retarded by ticket purchasing and the checking of baggage, should be entirely separated from the suburban passengers, who almost invariably pass direct from the street to the car without any delay in the station."

Wilgus came up with some of the earliest and most audacious plans for the terminal, and while these plans may have been more inspirational than practical, they shaped the future of the project. Among them was the concept of separate terminals for commuters (who made the trip each day and thus knew exactly what they were doing) and tourists (who were often coming into a confusing place and need more help). To accomplish this, he proposed that several stories of the colossal building be built below ground level.

A 1912 depiction of the ramp to the subway at Grand Central

As is often the case, the final consideration was the most important, at least in the sense of meeting the most immediate need. "Lastly, in view of the vast increase which must necessarily and rapidly take place in the future, the station must be built on a scale much larger than is absolutely needed by the present volume of travel; and this provision must extend not merely to the area devoted to passengers in waiting rooms, ticket lobbies, and concourse, but to the station yard itself, which must be extended in area to accommodate the larger number of trains that will be required."

In all, the writer for *Scientific American* was impressed with the plans and predicted that they would bring about success. He concluded, "Now, it must be admitted, after an impartial study of the plans of this great undertaking, that the above requirements appear to have been fully met and all the provision for the future made that can reasonably be asked. Architecturally, the station building will present a massive and dignified appearance, worthy of what is probably the most important railroad terminal in America. The architecture of the building is throughout and without exception an expression of the plan; none of the decoration being used merely for architectural effect, but everything serving some useful, structural purpose. Thus the main piers under the great arched roof of the concourse, and at the intersection of the roof and its transept, are necessary to carry the load of the massive steel work of the roof. This is true even of the two massive piers that flank the main entrance on Forty-Second Street, their great mass serving to take the horizontal thrust of the arches. The only possible exception is the pairs of columns between the arches of the Forty-second Street entrance; and these are placed there merely to accentuate the fact that this is the main approach. The proportions of the facade are truly monumental, the main arches being 33 feet in width by 60 feet in height, and the cornice being about 75 feet above the street level. The whole structure will be faced with gray granite, and with its great frontage of 300 feet on Forty-second Street and twice that distance on Vanderbilt Avenue, and with an open width of street of from 130 to 140 feet to afford a fitting point of view, it must long remain one of the most successful of the monumental buildings of New York City."

Indeed, there is so much granite in Grand Central Terminal that it will easily set off a well-calibrated Geiger counter.

Modern pictures of the exterior

Chapter 5: Electric Trains

The main concourse of Grand Central Station

Picture of a ballet performance held at Grand Central

"'Suddenly, there came a flash of light,' [Wilgus] recalled decades later. 'It was the most daring idea that ever occurred to me.' In a succinct three-page letter to W.H. Newman, the railroad's president, dated December 22, 1902, less than a year after the crash, the 37-year-old self-taught chief engineer recommended an audacious and extravagant remedy: raze the new Grand Central Station that had just been renovated and replace the egregious steam locomotives with electric trains, which had advanced technologically since they were first introduced on a main line by the Baltimore & Ohio in 1895 (four years later Wilgus himself had proposed an experimental trial on the Central; his plan was adopted but not implemented)." – Sam Roberts, *Grand Central: How a Train Station Transformed America*

In a turn of events that is all too rare for construction projects, electric trains began to run earlier than expected. In July 1906, *Scientific American* ran the enthusiastic headline "Early Opening of New York Central Electric Service," and those who took time to read the article were told that the "determination of the New York Central Company to hurry forward the installation of the electric service, at least through the Park Avenue tunnel, is highly commendable, and will be exceedingly welcome to everyone who has occasion to travel by way of that notorious two miles of discomfort. If one were to judge by the apparently backward condition of the new terminal itself, it would look as though the opening of the new electric service were yet many years removed; but the company has wisely determined not to wait upon the completion of the Grand Central Station. They propose to complete the excavation of the easterly half of the station yard; create a temporary terminal at the Grand Central Palace, and start the operation of trains by electric power over the first few miles of road out of the city, just as soon as the new power station at Port Morris Is in condition to supply the current."

Indeed, the article continued, "The time set for the opening of-.electrical service from the Grand Central Station to High Bridge on the main line, and to Wakefield on the Harlem division, is the middle of October. The laying of the third rail and placing of the cables is well on the way to completion…" The author then added that "already two of the 85-ton electric locomotives have been delivered, and they will be set in service on a stretch of experimental track at High Bridge, where the engineers will be broken in to their new duties as motormen." The sheer numbers of rail cars being added to the station were staggering: "One hundred and twenty-five steel electric motor cars and 55 trailers have been ordered, and the first installment will shortly be in the city."

Even more amazing was the power it would take to run the cars. The article explained, "At the Port Morris power house, one of the turbine generators has been put in operation, and another is nearly completed. By October 15th the divisions from Harlem and Wakefield to Forty-second Street will be in condition to commence active operation, and as the months pass by, the electrical equipment will be extended, both as regards the line and the rolling stock, without waiting for the completion of the great terminal station, whose construction can be carried forward without interference in the operation of the trains. The equipment of the New Haven system is also being pushed vigorously; the concrete piers for the towers which will carry the overhead line are nearly all in place, and the power station, which is being built at Cos Cob to supply the system from Woodlawn to Stamford, is now about one-half completed. The New Haven electric locomotives will use the overhead system from Stamford to Woodlawn, from which point into the Grand Central Station they will take current from the third rail of the New York Central system."

The first challenge facing the men building the new terminal was digging the footing for the foundation that would support the weight of the building and all the railroad tracks that ran through it. Revisiting the issue in September 1905, *Scientific American* observed, "One of the features that render the construction of the new Grand Central terminal station a work of unprecedented and monumental proportions, is the vast amount of preliminary excavation that has to be carried out before a single track of the station yard, or a single brick or stone of the station building can be laid. This excavation amounts to a total of over 2,000,000 cubic yards, a large part of which is rock. The blasting out and digging of this material in the heart of a great city, and its removal and disposal many miles from the point of excavation, is in itself a task of huge proportions."

In fact, the terminal's location made this situation particularly challenging. As the article pointed out, the soil being removed from the site could not simply be piled in a nearby empty lot but instead had to be hauled away by engines sitting on tracks already in place. Regardless, the work had to be done for the terminal to be built on the scale envisioned by its designers. The article continued, "The vast amount of excavation that is being done at the site of the new station is necessitated by the fact that the tracks, both of the terminal yard and in the station itself, will be carried on two levels, one above the other, and to the further fact that the whole of the double-decked terminal, as thus constructed, will be below street grade. The total- average depth of the excavation to sub-grade of the suburban tracks on the lower deck will be about 35 feet. The area to be excavated will extend the total width of Park Avenue for a distance of 1,700 feet from' Fiftieth to Forty-fifth Street, and it will extend from Vanderbilt Avenue to Lexington Avenue from Forty-fifth to Forty-second Street. The difficulty of the work will be more fully understood when it is mentioned that every cubic yard of the total of over 2,000,000 yards has to be taken out and removed through the four-track tunnel, which is the only means of access to the station, without interfering with the regular traffic of the road."

Chapter 6: The New Grand Central Terminal

"The new Grand Central Terminal— and it would be a terminal, because New York Central horse cars would no longer ferry commuters from its train platforms to destinations downtown— would draw nearly as many people in a single day as Times Square did on New Year's Eve. Grand Central was designed to accommodate even more, maybe even as many as 100 million a year by the beginning of the 21st century, when the terminal would celebrate its centennial. Even before the first spadeful of earth was turned, before the first boulder of Manhattan schist was blasted, a veritable forest of exclamation points began sprouting with what was dubbed the city's largest individual demolition contract ever. On 17 acres purchased by the railroad, 120 houses, three churches, two hospitals, and an orphan asylum would have to be obliterated, as would stables, warehouses, and other ancillary structures. The Times admitted that "in describing it, the superlative degree must be kept in constant use." It would be the biggest, it would contain the most trackage, and, on top of that, it would be self-supporting." – Sam Roberts, *Grand Central: How a Train Station Transformed America*

A picture of Grand Central in 1918

In spite of the recent accidents, the nature of the city itself demanded that most of the tracks in and out of the terminal be run underground, but *Scientific American* mentioned some of the improvements that could be made: "The entrance to the present and to the future terminal station is by way of the existing four-track tunnel, two miles in length, below Park Avenue. This tunnel will not be enlarged by the addition of more tracks, but its capacity for the regular passage of trains will be enormously enlarged for the reason that the storage yard for cars and engines will no longer be at Mott Haven, beyond the Harlem River, but will be located within the terminal yard itself. This means that the large number of empty trains that used to be taken out through the tunnel to Mott Haven for cleaning and overhauling, will remain in the terminal yard between trips, and the present congestion through the tunnel will be relieved to that extent, enabling a much larger number of regular daily passenger trains to be run through the tunnel in the twenty-four hours."

As noted before, the daily passenger trains were a significant concern because of the increasing number of commuters in the city. The article also addressed this issue: "Furthermore, the installation of electric traction will render the tunnel atmosphere clear, and will enable the trains to run under closer headway. The new station yards will commence at Fifty-Seventh Street, where the tunnel has been excavated out to the full width of Park Avenue — 140 feet. In order to enable the turnouts to be made without interference from supporting columns, a massive steel truss has been erected at this point for carrying the roof of the tunnel. Provision against accident at these turnouts is further secured by imbedding the lower half of the columns in continuous concrete walls. It is expected that if a derailment should at any time occur, these walls will serve as a shield to protect the columns, and also to prevent the telescoping or serious wrecking of the cars. This is a safety provision which we commend to the consideration of the builders of our future subways in this city, in which, at all curves, there should he similar continuous concrete walls between adjoining tracks. The 140-foot excavation will provide width for ten parallel tracks, which will be continued down to Fiftieth Street, where they will open out into the main yard, and occupy the space from Lexington Avenue to a line 100 feet east from Madison Avenue to Forty-Third Street, and thence to Forty-Second Street the station ground will be bounded by Vanderbilt Avenue on the west and for a shorter distance by Depew Place on the east."

One of the things that made constructing the Grand Central Terminal different from building Grand Central Depot was the assumption made by the builders that the city would continue to grow. This assumption was based not just on the city's history but also on the observations made by those in charge of the way in which commerce gravitated to anywhere that a new railroad station was built. Scientific American noted, "After the station yard has been completed, all the cross streets from Fifty-Seventh Street to the north face of the terminal station will be restored, and a driveway will be formed on each side of Park Avenue. From these streets and driveways it will be possible to look down upon the upper deck of the terminal yard. Ultimately, however, it is likely that the blocks bounded by these streets will be covered by buildings, thus entirely shutting in the station yard. Provisions for the footings of these buildings will be made during the construction of the terminal."

One of the many important changes that was made when constructing the new building was that the local commuter trains were thoroughly separated from the long distance trains. In fact, as the article pointed out, they were on completely different levels. "The tracks of the main or upper yard begin to drop at Fifty-Seventh Street, until they reach a level 15 feet below the grade of the present tracks. This level is continuous over the whole of the yard and through the terminal building. At Fifty-Third Street the two outermost of the ten tracks begin to drop on a two per cent grade to the level of the lower deck, which will be 35 feet below street grade. The excavation for the lower level for suburban trains will not extend over the full width of the yard throughout its entire length. This level will be provided in the station with fifteen parallel tracks, and in the station yard with thirty tracks. The lower deck excavation will be carried for its full width as far north as Forty-Eighth Street, whence it will narrow gradually to the point where it meets the two outermost suburban inclines, that lead up to the common level in the tunnel."

Picture of a ramp to a lower concourse

Not surprisingly, the biggest challenge was how to accomplish the changes that needed to be made while still maintaining train traffic through the terminal, and the designers managed this through careful planning. "The method of carrying through the work so as not to interfere with existing traffic will be to excavate for two or three tracks at the main yard or upper level, each side of the approach to the main yard, and put in a temporary station for the use of the suburban traffic on the easterly side of the yard. When this has been done a straight section will be excavated right down through the yard, and then the western section will be taken out. The lower level construction will be carried on conjointly with that of the main yard, or at least as far as it is possible to do so. The excavation is being done chiefly by steam shovel. The material is loaded directly on to flat cars, and is taken out through the tunnel, and used chiefly in widening the embankment of the New York Central roadbed sufficiently to provide for a fourth track from New York to Croton, a distance of 34 miles. There is also sufficient material for adding, if desired, a fifth or sixth track roadbed, while a large amount of the material has been used for filling in fifty or sixty acres of land belonging to the company at Highbridge marshes, ground which will be very serviceable for storage purposes."

Another concern that had be carefully considered was to make sure that the new tunnels being dug would not harm the foundations of the buildings they were going under. As the article pointed out, "The excavation of the station has called for some very careful work in underpinning the buildings that front on Park Avenue. ...an extensive piece of needle-beam work [was] put in to carry the weight of the Steinway piano factory, and is a fair sample of the difficulties encountered. The side walls of the excavation are formed of 15-inch vertical I-beams, placed 3 feet 6 inches' between centers, with concrete arches turned in between. The roof, forming the roadways of Park Avenue and the intersecting streets, is formed of 24-inch I-beams, with flooring of reinforced concrete or of buckleplate. ...the southerly facade extends for 300 feet on Forty-Second Street, and the westerly facade for 680 feet on Vanderbilt Avenue. The building will also have a frontage on Forty-Fifth Street of 625 feet, and on Lexington Avenue of 400 feet. The station will include a ticket lobby, 90 feet by 300 feet, and a grand concourse 160 feet by 470 feet in length, with a height from floor to top of dome roof of 150 feet."

Chapter 7: The Wellspring of New Beginnings

"Grand Central has been the wellspring of new beginnings for millions of people who arrived in New York to fulfill their dreams, heeded the siren call to go west, and returned lovesick to their hometowns. Unlike a station, a terminal conjures up a destination, not merely a place to pass through. Grand Central embodied that role, as the gateway to New York since 1913 and as the city's Gateway to a Continent. Between 1913 and the centennial of the New York Central in 1926, the number of passengers served annually by the terminal nearly doubled, to 43 million from 23 million. Today, the number is verging on a record, headed, for the first time, toward the 100 million passengers a year forecast when the terminal first opened a century ago." – Sam Roberts, *Grand Central: How a Train Station Transformed America*

Picture of the main waiting room

From the first day that it opened, Grand Central Terminal prided itself on being passenger friendly, assuring potential customers that they "may ask questions with no fear of being rebuffed by hurrying trainmen, or imposed upon by hotel runners, chauffeurs, or others in blue uniforms." The new terminal also promised that "walking encyclopedias" clad formally in dove colored coats and bright white caps could answer all questions. In fact, one brochure informed customers that they were coming to "a place where one delights to loiter, admiring its beauty and symmetrical lines— a poem in stone."

Puffery pieces aside, the new Grand Central was widely considered a massive improvement, and on February 2, 1913, *The New York Times* praised the builders in an article with the headline "Solving Greatest Terminal Problem of the Age." "In view of the many changes that the New York Central's terminal has undergone in the course of its history, people are asking, quite naturally, whether the great railroad station that is open to-day for the first time is the final, permanent structure, adequate to accommodate whatever future development may come to the great system of traffic to which it belongs...The new station had to be large enough. It also had to be convenient enough. It had to be roomy, but mere roominess would not serve the purpose. In a sense, the very size of the terminal threatened to be a drawback. It must not be too large or seem too large for easy use. The architects set before themselves the problem of planning a station that would be as compact as the little station of a little town. In a sense then, the new Grand Central Terminal was planned to be one of the 'smallest' big stations in the world."

Unfortunately, some visitors were more welcome than others, but this was considered a benefit at the time. One newspaper article explained, "Special accommodations are to be provided for immigrants and gangs of laborers. They can be brought into the station and enter a separate room without meeting other travelers." They were being intentionally kept away from wealthier visitors, many of whom were staying at the newly built Commodore Hotel. Others subsequently worked at the nearby Chrysler Building, which itself was a product of the fact that by the time Grand Central Terminal was completed, the real estate surrounding it had already been purchased by men planning to turn the area into a new bastion of upscale life.

Naturally, one of the reasons so many people wanted to live near the newly built terminal was that it made it easy to get to so many other places in the city. *The Times* explained, "One of the most conspicuous features of the terminal plans was the obvious effort to systematize every activity with which henceforth it will be astir. Everything is segregated. When the thing is all done there will be a separate and distinct station for the incoming and outgoing passengers. These stations will be all part of one structure, of course, and it will be the simplest thing in the world to get from one to the other. But they will be distinct. The incoming folk will not meet the outgoing. More important than that, they will not run into one another...As the last word in segregation, consider the announcement that even sentiment is to be segregated in the new Grand Central Terminal. There are specially designed parts of the station known as the 'Kissing Galleries.' They are the places where you may go to meet the person you want to meet. These galleries run alongside the inclined walks on which the stream of passengers from a train just arrived make their way to the street. Slightly elevated, it is promised that they will offer exceptional vantage points for recognition, hailing, and the subsequent embrace. Time was when the embracing went on all over the terminal and the indignant handlers of the baggage trucks would swear that their paths were forever being blocked by leisurely demonstrations of affection. But we have changed all that."

The day after the new terminal opened, the *Christian Science Monitor* noted, "First remarked in the new Grand Central is the main concourse on the upper level. This huge auditorium, running the entire width of the main structure, with its center line coinciding exactly with Forty-Third Street, is 300 feet long, 125 feet wide and 125 feet high, and finished in Botticini marble.... The use of electricity in place of steam for motive power in the new terminal has made the tarnished of the new Grand Central entirely different from that of the earlier station. The electric locomotive has made possible economy of space at the new terminal and the yards and platform tracks have been placed beneath street surfaces with baggage and other facilities grouped above them. The absolute separation of inward and outward-bound passengers is another feature of the efficiency of the new terminal."

Modern photo of the main concourse

That first day, the terminal was put to its first big test. According to *The Times*, "More than 150,000 persons, railroad officials estimated, visited the new Grand Central Terminal between midnight yesterday when the doors were opened to the public and at 7 o'clock last night. This vast throng, railroad men declared, was made up principally of people from Manhattan, Brooklyn and the Bronx. Hundreds of persons remained in the great concourse throughout the early morning hours, and from 8 o'clock yesterday morning until 5 in the afternoon, the main floor of the concourse and the galleries were packed with the visitors. It was a curious, good-natured throng and reached its height at 4 o'clock, when the great structure was so crowded that persons found difficulty in moving. Railroad men viewed the scene with amazement, saying that never before had the public been known to take such a keen interest in the opening of a railroad terminal."

Indeed, this interest was just the beginning. Terminal City, as the area around Grand Central came to be called, soon became the home of many new buildings. The 34 story Helmsley

Building, located just north of the terminal, was completed in 1928 and became headquarters for the New York Central Railroad. In 1922, the famed Grand Central Art Gallery opened, and a few years later, author Walter Clark wrote of it, "While the question and method of establishing the galleries was still merely an idea, [famed artist John Singer] Sargent was the first painter who was seriously approached for advice in the matter. A pleasant dinner and an evening was spent with him for the express purpose of talking the matter over. His keen sympathy was at once aroused and his constructive suggestions were most ardent and helpful. Many were in the form of friendly criticism and his mind went over the problem in all its probable future conditions. It is interesting now to remember how many of his predictions have come true in our experience since the galleries were actually put into operation. After going over the subject for several hours, Mr. Sargent arose and said, 'Now, I have thought of all the difficulties that I could, but really they do not amount to anything and I am for going ahead and putting it through.' And from that time until his death never once was there a time when he did not respond promptly and generously to every request that was made of him in the interest of the undertaking. One of the arrangements in the founding of the Grand Central Gallery was that each artist-member was to give to the organization a picture or a bronze each year for three years. Mr. Sargent's first picture was called 'An Artist Sketching,' and the gallery had an offer of $5,000 for it before the distribution to lay-members took place. One of his other contributions has recently been put on the market at a price of $10,000. These were prizes won by our lay members. Mr. Sargent's name helped materially in promoting the undertaking on the broad lines in which it had been conceived."

Walter Clark (left) at a 1933 event in Grand Central

Sargent

Entrance to the Grand Central Art Galleries

From its inception, those building the terminal always assumed that dignitaries from around the state and around the world would visit from time to time, so they installed a number of "secret" platforms, rooms and staircases for their use. One of these, 61, was designed to allow the famous to make their way from the terminal to the nearby Waldorf-Astoria Hotel without ever going outside, and Franklin Roosevelt used this platform a number of times during his presidency. William Hassett, one of Roosevelt's secretaries, discussed one of these occasions: "The speech over with, a Secret Service agent rescued Grace Tully and me from the throng of diners and we went down in the hotel elevator with the President and Mrs. Roosevelt to the spur track which was put in at the construction of the new Waldorf-Astoria for the accommodation of the private cars of 'economic royalists'— never, however, used but twice: once by General Pershing when he was ill, and now, of all persons, by the arch-foe of the privileged group for whose delectation this extravagant convenience was devised. Another irony of fate. The wheel has come full circle. We were soon out from under the Waldorf and on our way to Hyde Park."

Chapter 8: A Flawed Symbol of Civic Pride

A picture of the Ladies' Room in Grand Central

"'Through the old grand central, 21 million passengers passed to and fro last year,' The Times gushed just before the new terminal opened in 1913. 'Owing to the perfection of the new arrangement, five times as many, or more than the whole population of the United States, can be handled just as easily in 12 months.' Initially, the terminal was criticized as being too big for any traffic demand that could ever be made upon it. Now, a century later, Grand Central is finally nearing the 100 million passengers annually projected when it opened—instead of falling victim to its own success as what The Times' Herbert Muschamp called 'a flawed symbol of civic pride.' During the 1990s renovation, he wrote, the terminal seemed to be 'in effect, a double agent,' because 'while undeniably a great urban landmark, it is also a monument to the centrifugal forces— first trains, then cars, now modems— that since the 1920s have hastened the suburban exodus of the middle class." – Sam Roberts, *Grand Central: How a Train Station Transformed America*

In addition to its more elegant tenants, Grand Central Terminal was also the home of the first CBS television station beginning in 1939. Later, in 1958, it housed the world's first videotaping facility. Don Hewitt, who went on to create the famous news show *60 Minutes*, recalled, "They had cameras and lights and makeup artists and stage managers and microphones just like in the movies, and I was hooked. I had been passing through Grand Central every day on my way to work and never knew that upstairs, over the trains and the waiting room and the information booth, was an attic stuffed with the most fabulous toys anyone ever had to play with. I was mesmerized. As a child of the movies, I was torn between wanting to be Julian Marsh, the Broadway producer in '42nd Street,' who was up to his ass in showgirls, and Hildy Johnson, the hell-bent-for-leather reporter in 'The Front Page,' who was up to his ass in news stories. Oh my God, I thought, in television I could be both of them."

In spite of its upscale features, Grand Central Terminal was not kept up very well through the years, and by the time World War II was over, it was badly in need of a facelift. At the same time, cross country train travel was waning and the terminal was becoming increasingly dependent on local commuters to make ends meet. This didn't bring in big money, which compelled some to call for changes if not an outright replacement. In 1954, developer William Zeckendorf began a short-lived campaign to replace the terminal with an 80 story skyscraper that would be 500 feet taller than the Empire State Building, and even though his plans fell through, some were nervous about the terminal's future. In 1960, author E. B. White wrote, "I live in the twilight of railroading, the going down of its sun. For the past few months I've been well aware that I am the Unwanted Passenger, one of the last survivors of a vanishing and ugly breed. Indeed, if I am to believe the statements I see in the papers, I am all that stands between the Maine railroads and a bright future of hauling fast freight for a profit."

In 1963, Erwin Wolfson completed work on the Pan Am Building (later the Met Life Building) just north of the terminal, but the income generated by Grand Central was still not living up to its potential. Thus, in 1968, there was another plan put forward to build a tower or new structure over the terminal. The previous year, the city had declared the terminal a historic landmark, blocking any further changes to it, but the owners of the terminal, Penn Central Transportation, appealed. The debate eventually compelled former First Lady Jacqueline Kennedy Onassis to weigh in: "Is it not cruel to let our city die by degrees, stripped of all her proud monuments, until there will be nothing left of all her history and beauty to inspire our children? If they are not inspired by the past of our city, where will they find the strength to fight for her future? Americans care about their past, but for short term gain they ignore it and tear down everything that matters. Maybe… this is the time to take a stand, to reverse the tide, so that we won't all end up in a uniform world of steel and glass boxes."

People were more than happy to rally around her, and a few months later, according to Nina Gershon (who represented them), "There were some in the preservation community who questioned the city's resolve to pursue, through appeal, the fight to preserve Grand Central Terminal as a landmark, after a devastating loss in the trial court, which had not only rejected, with derision, the findings of the Landmarks Preservation Commission regarding the significance of the Terminal but found that the designation of the Terminal as a landmark was unconstitutional; ominously, the trial court had also severed and kept open the request for damages for a "temporary taking." But when [attorney Bernie Richland] became convinced of the merit of the city's position, he did not stint in his support of the appeal."

The case in question, *Penn Central Transportation Co. v. New York City* (1978), made history by being the first case the Supreme Court ever took concerning historic preservation. The high court found in favor of preservation, ruling that the designation of Grand Central as a landmark did not constitute a "taking" of it from Penn Central Transportation. The terminal remains a historic landmark to this day.

A little over a decade after the Supreme Court ruling, a group of art historians released a report on the terminal in which they concluded, "Viewed urbanistically, Grand Central Terminal is without parallel. The urban design of the vast building vitalized and embraced its broader surroundings. Accommodating the city, the Terminal provided a circumferential roadway which circled it, underground passages which linked to buildings beyond it, corridors and ramps which led one through it, and tunnels for trains and subways to stop beneath it. The interior comfort and dignity of the traveler and commuter was of paramount consideration in the design of Grand Central Terminal. The elegant finishes and spatial quality throughout created a unified setting with a restful palette of neutral colors. The stark elegance of the uncluttered marble and stone walls and simple black-letter signs, the clarity of the programming and spaces, and the efficiency of the many services and amenities all serve the architect's original intent that the building 'is not to be an art museum, or a hall of fame, but a place of dignified simplicity, easy of access and comfortable.' Grand Central Terminal was the consummate civic monument —and yet it was even more. Commercially it stood as one of America's first multi -use buildings, incorporating shops, restaurants, stores and offices— in short, all the diversity of a city within the confines of one building."

In 1998, after some major renovations, an article in *The New Yorker* proclaimed, "The real brilliance of the place —for all its architectural glory— is the way in which it confirms the virtues of the urban ensemble. Grand Central was conceived as the monumental center of a single composition, with hotels and streets and towers and subways arrayed around it. When it opened, in 1913, it was New York's clearest embodiment of the essential urban idea— that different kinds of buildings work together to make a whole that is far greater than any of its parts. If Penn Station was built mainly to send a message about the splendor of arrival, then Grand Central was conceived to make clear the choreography of connection."

While the opinion of architectural historians and popular magazines is valuable, Grand Central Depot and Grand Central Terminal were ultimately built for the people, so it is perhaps best left to someone who has lived with it for years to have the final word on its value. In 1998, New York author Lee Stringer wrote, "When I first saw Grand Central Terminal close to 40 years ago— headed upstate with my mother and brother to visit Aunt Lillian—it was the quintessential public building, an astoundingly democratic place. The porters, Red Caps and conductors all treated us like first-class passengers, though we were traveling the equivalent of steerage. Twenty-odd years later, penniless, I ended up living in Grand Central, along with hundreds of homeless New Yorkers. It has since struck me how perfectly right it was that a great public building should serve, above everything else, as a refuge— in my case for 10 years. Grand Central was anything but beautiful or elegant the winter I first staked out a niche on its lower levels— and certainly not grand. But in the thousand small acts of kindness tendered then by busy, bustling New Yorkers— acts as small as an encouraging word— I detected a whisper of the indomitable spirit that distinguishes this from any other mere compilation of brick and mortar that dares call itself a city. That New York, no matter what the human condition, shrugged and said: 'It's cold. Come inside.'"

Bibliography

Belle, John; Leighton, Maxinne Rhea (2000). *Grand Central: Gateway to a Million Lives*. New York: Norton.

Federal Writers' Project (1982). *The WPA Guide to New York City: The Federal Writers' Project Guide to 1930s New York*. New York: Pantheon Books.

Middleton, William D. (1999). *Grand Central, the World's Greatest Railway Terminal*. San Marino: Golden West Books.

Roberts, Sam (2013). *Grand Central: How a Train Station Transformed America*. Grand Central Publishing. Kindle Edition.

Schlichting, Kurt C. (2001). *Grand Central Terminal: Railroads, Architecture and Engineering in New York*. Baltimore: Johns Hopkins University Press.

CPSIA information can be obtained at www.ICGtesting.com
Printed in the USA
LVOW10s1814150216

475194LV00027B/1322/P